William Lloyd Birkbeck

Historical Sketch of the Distribution of Land in England

with suggestions for some improvement in the law

William Lloyd Birkbeck

Historical Sketch of the Distribution of Land in England
with suggestions for some improvement in the law

ISBN/EAN: 9783337096700

Printed in Europe, USA, Canada, Australia, Japan

Cover: Foto ©ninafisch / pixelio.de

More available books at **www.hansebooks.com**

HISTORICAL SKETCH

OF THE

DISTRIBUTION OF LAND
IN ENGLAND

WITH

Suggestions for some Improvement in the Law

BY

WILLIAM LLOYD BIRKBECK, M.A.

MASTER OF DOWNING COLLEGE, AND
DOWNING PROFESSOR OF THE LAWS OF ENGLAND IN THE UNIVERSITY OF CAMBRIDGE

London
MACMILLAN AND CO.
1885

[*The Right of Translation and Reproduction is Reserved*]

CONTENTS.

PART I.

		PAGE
I.	ANGLO-SAXON AGRICULTURE—GENEATS AND GEBURS—VILLANI	1
II.	AGRICULTURE AFTER THE CONQUEST—VILLENAGE—COPYHOLDERS—CONTINENTAL SERFS	5
III.	ORIGIN OF LARGE PROPERTIES—ESTATES OF ANGLO-SAXON NOBILITY—EVIDENCE OF DOMESDAY	8
IV.	THE SOKE—SOCAGE TENURE	14
V.	AGRICULTURAL COMMUNITIES IN NASSE	17
VI.	MR. SEEBOHM	22
VII.	THE FIRST TAXATION OF LAND—THE HIDE	25
VIII.	SAXON LAW OF SUCCESSION TO LAND	29
IX.	EFFECT OF THE NORMAN CONQUEST ON THE DISTRIBUTION OF LAND	33
X.	NORMAN LAW OF SUCCESSION	38
XI.	STRICT ENTAILS—THE STATUTE "DE DONIS CONDITIONALIBUS"	43

		PAGE
XII.	EFFECTS OF STRICT ENTAILS—SCOTCH ENTAILS	48
XIII.	RELAXATION OF STRICT ENTAILS—COMMON RECOVERIES	54
XIV.	HENRY VII. AND HIS NOBLES—THE STATUTE OF FINES	58
XV.	STRICT SETTLEMENTS	61
XVI.	EFFECT OF STRICT SETTLEMENTS OF LAND—MR. THOROLD ROGERS	66
XVII.	TRUSTEES TO PRESERVE CONTINGENT REMAINDERS	70
XVIII.	POWERS OF SALE	74
XIX.	INCLOSURE OF WASTE LANDS—MR. JOHN WALTER—FORMATION OF A PEASANT PROPRIETARY	77

PART II.

I.	AMENDMENT OF LAW OF PRIMOGENITURE	82
II.	PROPOSED SYSTEM OF REGISTRATION	85
III.	MODERN REGISTRATION ACTS	90
IV.	THE PRESENT GENERAL REGISTRATION ACT	92

HISTORICAL SKETCH

OF THE

DISTRIBUTION OF LAND IN ENGLAND.

I.

ANGLO-SAXON AGRICULTURE.—GENEATS AND GEBURS.
VILLANI.

THE changes that take place in the terms on which land is held, and the manner in which it is cultivated, are usually so gradual that they escape the notice of contemporaries. The causes of such changes thus become at a subsequent period matters of conjecture, giving rise not unfrequently, as we shall have occasion to point out, to most extravagant theories.

The first period at which we obtain any detailed account of the agricultural condition of England is that which succeeded, at no great interval, the Norman Conquest. The admirable survey made by order of William I., the record of which is preserved in the two volumes known by the popular name of *Domesday Book*, stands unrivalled (so far as I am aware) by any memorial respecting the material and social condition of this or any other country.

Before adverting to the conclusions which may be drawn from the great survey, it will be convenient to refer shortly to the scanty information we possess respecting earlier times, so far as it throws light upon the terms and statements of *Domesday*.

In the *Rectitudines Singularum Personarum* (*Ancient Laws and Institutes of England*, 1840. Vol. i. 431), a short treatise in Saxon and Latin, of uncertain date, but which from internal evidence we may safely conclude was composed in Saxon times, we find described the duties of the various classes of owners and occupiers of land.

Thus the thegn, or landowner, is obliged to serve the king in war, and to assist in making or repairing fortified places and bridges. This is the *trinoda necessitas*, so often a subject of complaint with Anglo-Saxon proprietors.

The duties of the geneats are to till, to sow, and reap the land of their lord, to go on errands far and near for him, to provide a horse, to fell wood for his deer park, to perform other servile works, and to make certain small payments in money or kind.

The gebur, when he enters on his "yard of land,"

is to be supplied with two oxen, one cow, and six sheep, and seven acres of his land are to be sown for him. After the first year he must perform the duties attached to his condition. In some places he must work two days in each week, in harvest (rendered in the Latin text Augustus) three days. He is to plough one acre a week from the time when ploughing begins till Martinmas. He also makes small payments in money and kind. If he departs (dies), all that he has belongs to his lord.

These general rules were subject (as appears by the same document) to some variation, dependent on the custom of the district in which the lands were situate.

There can, I think, be no question that the cultivation of the soil, when the *Rectitudines* were written, was mainly carried on by the geneats and geburs. They were evidently not slaves whose duties depended absolutely on the will of their lord. Their work was defined by the general custom, as described in the *Rectitudines*, subject to variation by the local custom of the district. Of these two classes the geneats were legally unfree; and the geburs, by their poverty, must have been practically in a servile condition, even if not unfree according to law.

If we turn now to the Great Record, we shall, I think, find that the course of husbandry had suffered little alteration from the change in regard to the ownership of land which, in many cases, had taken place during the interval of twenty years between the Conquest and the completion of *Domesday*.

The properties mentioned in *Domesday* are generally styled *villæ* or *maneria*, and had usually, before the Conquest, been the property of Saxon nobles, or were then, and still remained, the property of ecclesiastics, or of the Crown; and almost invariably attached to the villa are a certain number of *villani*. Now the word *villanus* occurs in the Latin text of the *Rectitudines* as the equivalent of the Saxon geneat. In *Domesday* it probably included the gebur also, the distinction between the two in the *Rectitudines* not being very apparent.

The *villani*, afterwards called the *villeins* by the Norman lawyers, were men allowed, like the geburs of the *Rectitudines*, to occupy small allotments, or "yards," of land for the support of themselves and their families, and who, in return, were required to plough, sow, and reap the land which their lord kept in his own hands—his *demesne*, as it was called.

II.

AGRICULTURE AFTER THE CONQUEST.—VILLENAGE. —COPYHOLDERS.—CONTINENTAL SERFS.

It appears from the authorities to which I have referred, that both before and after the Conquest, at least a large portion of the agricultural population of England, was organised in the same manner, as that which prevailed over the greatest part of the Western European Continent, during the middle ages, and in some countries, as in Prussia, Poland and Hungary, almost to the present day; whilst in England, on the other hand, all traces of villenage have disappeared for centuries.

The main cause which occasioned the discontinuance of villenage in England, at a much earlier period than that at which it ceased to exist in foreign countries was probably economical.

The services due to the lord from the villein, peasant, bauer, or serf, as he was usually termed on the Continent, often a source of vexation to both parties, were, in England, at an early period, for the most part, commuted for an annual money payment; and so powerful was the influence of custom, that it came to be established law, that the villein, if he rendered his accustomed rent and other services, if any, in respect of his holding, could not be ejected from it, nor could his rent or services be increased. He obtained, by custom, fixity of rent and fixity of tenure.

A list was kept of these tenants on the estate and their holdings by the steward of the owner, and at every change of a tenant, the fact was notified at a court or assembly of tenants held under the presidency of the steward, and an entry on this list or roll became evidence of the right of the tenant to hold his land. A copy of the entry was given to him, and he was said to hold his land by copy of court-roll; but tolerably conclusive evidence of the original infirmity of his title, was preserved in his legal designation, which was, and still is, "tenant *at the will of the lord*, by copy of court roll, according to the custom of the manor."

The disappearance of the class which in England corresponded to the peasantry of the Continent has been much deplored by some politicians. I will not stop to inquire whether it was a desirable state of things, that the agricultural proprietors should be sharply divided into two classes, having distinct customs, interests and opinions, as has been usually, if not invariably, the case, wherever peasant proprietors, properly so called, have existed. But I would remark that the disappearance of the English peasantry, "the divorce of the labourer from the soil," as it has been termed, is not due to oppression, but to prosperity. By the great fall in the value of silver, which commenced in the fifteenth century, the copyholder, who enjoyed by custom fixity of rent and tenure, became, in fact, a proprietor of his allotment, subject to some moderate burdens; and he therefore generally ceased to be a tiller of the soil. Cultivation came to be carried on universally by hired labourers, employed by copyholders as well as by freeholders. If injustice has been done in the course of this great change, it has certainly not been exercised by the owners of land on the peasantry, since a vast part of the best lands, to which the former were legally entitled, have become the property of the latter, without any equivalent being given by them, through the gradual operation of the causes to which I have alluded. Without revolution, and almost imperceptibly, landlordism was virtually abolished over at least one-fourth of the arable land of England. The burdens and restrictions to which copyhold lands remained subject, render them, no doubt, somewhat less valuable than freeholds of the same extent, but the difference is not generally of great importance.

III.

ORIGIN OF LARGE PROPERTIES.—ESTATES OF ANGLO-SAXON NOBILITY.—EVIDENCE OF DOMESDAY.

It is a commonly received opinion, that the present distribution of land in England differs greatly from that which prevailed in ancient, and particularly in Saxon times; and that the change is due to the operation of the law of primogeniture, or entail, or the practice of making settlements of land. I propose to consider in the first place, how far this opinion, that a great change in the distribution of land has occurred is well founded, before inquiring into the causes alleged to have produced it.

In order to arrive at a sound conclusion on the subject, we must extend the investigation into centuries long anterior to the Norman Conquest.

According to all historical accounts, the Saxon Conquest of England was effected by a body of men, about as insignificant in point of numbers, as the Spanish invaders of Mexico. A few long boats are said to have conveyed Hengist and his companions—conquerors of England. They were, no doubt, reinforced, and supported by a large immigration of their countrymen; but still after deducting those who fell in the struggle with the Romanised Britons, the residue must have formed a scanty band, when considered in connection with the extent of territory which lay at their disposal. They, however, were the ancestors of the kings and Saxon nobility of England. Is it to be supposed that these conquerors first ravaged the open country, and then began to cultivate it, in small properties, with their own hands? Is it not more probable, that the principal men among them took possession of the Roman villas, with which the country was studded, and cultivated the land like their immediate predecessors, by means of forced labour? I find no reason for holding, that the Saxon invaders of England differed greatly from the Germans as described by Tacitus—strenuous in war, slothful in peace. "Nec arare terram, aut expectare annonam, tam facile persuaseris, quam vocare hostes et vulnera mereri: pigrum quinimmo et iners videtur sudore adquirere quod possis sanguine parare."—*Germania*, cap. 14.

All conquerors and colonists bring with them their own laws and customs. Now, in Germany, the land was cultivated, according to the same testimony of Tacitus, by men who were not free, though not, like the Roman slaves, in a state of absolute bondage; the German serfs having separate dwellings and occupying portions of land, whilst rendering a return in kind to their lords. He says (after speaking of those who become slaves by staking their liberty in gambling), "Cæteris servis, non in nostrum morem, descriptis per familias, utuntur: suam quisque sedem, suos penates regit. Frumenti modum dominius, aut pecoris, aut vestis, ut colono injungit: et servi hactenus parent. . . . Verberare servum ac vinculis et opere coercere rarum."—TACITUS, *Germ.* cap. 25.

Why should we suppose that a people so tenacious of ancient habits as the Germans, introduced into England a system of cultivation unknown in Germany? We find serfdom existing in England, soon after the Norman Conquest, under the name of villenage; we find serfs in Saxon times under the designation of geneats or geburs; we find serfdom forming part of the German agricultural system in the days of Tacitus. Is there not, at least, a strong probability that the first-mentioned custom was derived from the last? Would the German warriors become more inclined to follow the plough, when they had the larger part of England at their disposal, than they were in their native country?

What then was there to prevent the Anglo-Saxon invaders, few in numbers as they were, from appropriating large tracts of country and cultivating them, however imperfectly, by serfs brought from Germany, or drawn from the inhabitants of the conquered lands? Bondage in one form or other was, we know, rife among the Anglo-Saxons.

Again, the quantity of land held sufficient for an Anglo-Saxon family was called a hide. Now the average hide cannot be estimated at less than 200 acres—a quantity obviously greater than that which could be cultivated by the owner and his family alone. The work was, in all probability, done by geneat or gebur labour. There is no reason to suppose that the Anglo-Saxons were less inclined to employ forced labour, than the Dutch were a few years ago (if not at present) in the Transvaal.

But whilst the hide appears to have been the minimum allotment, we meet with constant allusions in Anglo-Saxon laws and documents, to proprietors of five, of twenty, and even a much greater number of hides.

There is therefore, strong reason for believing that in the earliest Saxon period, there were proprietors of very large estates; and, as soon as the light of history breaks upon us, it reveals their existence. Etheldreda, an Anglian princess, in the seventh century, gave, it is said, the Isle of Ely to the abbey which she established. The Ealdorman Edric, in the days of Ethelred the Unready, could turn the scale in the struggle for supremacy between the Danes and the English. The manors of Earl Godwin are said to have stretched almost continuously through the county of Sussex. *Domesday Book* shows that the Earls Morcar, Edwin and Tosti (the brother of Harold) had vast possessions. In Cambridgeshire

"Œdiva Pulchra" held many manors at the Conquest. In Dorsetshire, as Mr. Eyton, in his admirable introduction to the *Domesday of the County*,[1] observes, Marlswayn was ubiquitous. The manor of Tewkesbury was held by Brictric and was estimated at ninety-five hides, not less probably than 20,000 acres. The Manor of Helston, in Cornwall, which belonged to Harold as Earl of the county, was of yet greater extent.

It is, therefore, I think, sufficiently obvious that vast estates existed in England from the earliest to the latest Anglo-Saxon days.

Extensive as were these possessions, it is not to be supposed that their owners were wealthy, in the modern acceptation of the word. The rent of land at the date of Domesday is estimated by Mr. Eyton at a penny an acre, a hide at a pound of silver, about £2 10*s.* 0*d.* of our present money, per annum.

On the other hand, the instruments of agriculture were dear, when compared with the rent of land. In Magna Carta, Cap. 21 (1225), the hire "limited of old" of a cart with two horses is 10*d.* a day, of a cart with three horses 1*s.* 2*d.*

Taking these facts into consideration, and remembering that the whole burden of the military establishment, of repairing fortified places, bridges and roads, was thrown upon the land, whilst the

---

[1] *Analysis of the Dorset Survey*, by the Rev. R. W. Eyton, 1877. See pp. 5*n*, 10.

means of communication were very imperfect, it is clear that few laymen, however extensive their manors might be, could have enjoyed a considerable surplus income, although they might command the necessaries of life in abundance—a condition in which many great landowners on the Continent still find themselves at the present day.

With the ecclesiastics the case was different. Their personal expenses were comparatively small, and when their possessions were considerable, they could devote large sums, not only to building stately monasteries and cathedrals, but also to increasing their revenues by bringing waste land into cultivation.

The lavish grants made to ecclesiastics may be explained, in part, by the fact that, in the hands of their donors, they were, through want of capital, comparatively worthless; and a landowner might, by means of a small sacrifice, become a great benefactor. Some persons appear to imagine that the early occupiers of land obtained, at once, a very valuable possession, forgetful that some of the best land in the world may, even at this day, be purchased in fee simple, for the cost of surveying it. But land is an insatiable devourer of capital. The amount annually expended on it may be small, but it becomes immense in the course of ages; and it is probable that few increments of value are better earned, than that which accrues to agricultural land in the course of many generations.

IV.

THE SOKE.—SOCAGE TENURE.

ALTHOUGH the properties mentioned in *Domesday* are generally considerable, and often very large, notices of smaller possessions, held by freemen, are not infrequent. The owners are usually said to be the men, *homines*, of some Saxon or Norman noble, and are termed socmanni, sokemen. The word soke at this time signified jurisdiction, and a landowner who, by prescription, or grant from the sovereign, was entitled to hold a court of justice, was said to have a soke. His men, that is the freemen who acknowledged that he was their lord—for he of whom another was man, was styled his lord—were legally bound to attend the Court of Justice held in the hall of the lord's residence, and, if not themselves parties, plaintiffs or defendants, to decide on matters arising within the limits of the soke.

The existence of these private jurisdictions was a matter almost of necessity, since without them, remote districts, from the feebleness of the state judicial institutions, and the difficulties of communication, would have been left without effectual legal supervision. Free landowners, who did not belong to a soke, were obliged to attend the Court of the Hundred; the hundred being a division of the county, generally of considerable extent. Such owners were styled simply freemen, *liberi homines*, or *liberi tenentes;* but their position differed from that of the sokemen merely as regarded the tribunal which they were bound to attend, and their being or not being under the protection of a lord. Hence, when a new free tenure, the military, was introduced, and it became necessary to discriminate the new from the old free tenures, the term socage tenure seems to have been extended to the freemen who owed service to the hundred court, although a public court, and was no longer confined, as in *Domesday*, to those who attended the court of a private person. The socmen are frequently mentioned in *Domesday* as bound to furnish inward— that is, to perform the duty of a local guard or watch. They probably formed the rank and file of the Saxon armies.

It is also probable that the smaller sokemen and free tenants, cultivated their lands themselves; but, judging from the *Domesday* record, I think we must conclude, that the total extent of land in the hands of small free proprietors, was insignificant, when compared with that which was cultivated by means of serf labour.

The terms on which the sokemen held their lands, as appears by *Domesday*, were various. Some could alienate their land without the license of their lord; others were unable to do so. If they possessed the right of alienation, in some instances, upon alienation, the jurisdiction over the land, the soke, remained with the lord; in other cases the tenants were free to dispose not only of the land, but of the soke also.

This variety seems to indicate that the relation of lord and sokeman often had its origin in contract. The liberated serf also must frequently have passed into the ranks of the sokemen. The latter generally paid a rent to his lord in money or in kind, as well in return for the protection he could claim, as for the use of his land. There are still freehold lands held of the lords of some manors, at ancient rents of small amount—generally called quit-rents.

When we consider the extraordinary deference which the Anglo-Saxon laws paid to wealth, estimating not only the value of a man's life, but the value of his testimony also, by the number of his hides, it is not difficult to account for the readiness, with which small free proprietors commended themselves to a great noble or prelate, and became his sokemen, in order to obtain his advocacy.

V.

AGRICULTURAL COMMUNITIES.

NOTWITHSTANDING that the facts I have mentioned are well known and rest, for the most part, on unquestionable authority, there is, I think, a current opinion that, during Anglo-Saxon times, land in England was, generally speaking, in the hands of free peasant proprietors—men who cultivated the soil with their own hands, for their own profit and were not subject to any master.

This opinion has received confirmation from a work on the *Agricultural Communities of the Middle Ages in England*, by E. Nasse, a German writer of considerable learning. The author maintains that communities of free peasant proprietors prevailed in England during the Anglo-Saxon period.

The author has, however, fallen into some important errors with regard to facts, and the conclusions which he draws from facts are not always incontrovertible.

His theory is founded, in a great measure, on the

continued existence of certain common rights in England up to recent times: the nature of these rights being recorded in the "Report of the Select Committee on Commons Inclosures appointed by the House of Commons in 1844," and the descriptions of Agriculture in the several counties of England published by the then Board of Agriculture, under the control of Sir John Sinclair, at the close of the last and commencement of the present century.

Thus he says at p. 3 of the translation made under the auspices of the Cobden Club :—

"The professional experts who were examined before the Committee in 1844 agreed in their information that, in many parts of the country, plots of arable land in the same township lay intermixed and uninclosed, so that the lands of a rural property consisted of narrow parcels lying scattered in a disconnected manner all over the extent of the village district (Dorfflur). These arable parcels were for the separate use of individual possessors from seedtime to harvest, after which they were open and common to all for pasturage. They were designated 'open commonable intermixed fields,' and also 'lammas lands,' because 'lammas' is the festival '*Petri ad vincula*' on the 1st of August—or, according to the old calendar by which the reckoning was then taken, the 13th of August—which was the period at which the common rights of pasture commenced."—(Nasse on the *Agricultural Com-*

munity of the Middle Ages, translated by Colonel H. A. Ouvry, p. 3.)

Now the period from "seed-time to harvest" never can have terminated in England, as a general rule, so early as the 13th of August. August is mentioned as harvest-time in ancient records (as in the *Rectitudines Singularum Personarum*, see above p. 3), and is still the harvest month in England. If the cattle had been turned upon the cultivated lands on the 13th of that month (as Nasse imagines they were), the destruction of the wheat- and other grain-crops must, in ordinary years, have been the consequence. Besides, in Anglo-Saxon times the error in the length of the Julian year had not occasioned (as Nasse seems to suppose) a difference of twelve days between the solar year and the calendar. If we take A.D. 750 as the mean year of the Saxon period, the difference would be only four days. So that the Saxon 1st of August would then correspond not with our present 13th, but our 5th of August—a date when the cutting of wheat- and other grain-crops has not commenced, in ordinary years, through a great part of England. In point of fact, the lands subject to this custom described by Nasse were not arable, but *meadow*; and they were inclosed not from "seed-time to harvest," but until the second hay-crop had been mown. The lands known as Lammas Lands at the present day are, I believe, invariably meadow.

If any confirmation of the fact be wanting, it may be found in the circumstance, that the only probable derivation of Lammas is Late-Math, late mowing. Hence "Latter Lammas," a later math than Lammas, became proverbial, as an equivalent to the Greek Calends.

Then the hypothesis that the cultivators of intermixed patches of land were free proprietors to whom, as a community, the land belonged, seems to rest upon two circumstances—first, that they all cultivated the land according to the same course of husbandry; and secondly, that they were entitled in common to depasture their cattle upon the land, after the crop had been removed.

Now, where land is held in small portions, and cultivated by the plough, the course of husbandry cannot, it is obvious, conveniently vary from one plot to another. The Anglo-Saxon plough was a cumbrous and costly instrument. It was drawn by eight oxen. The ancient measures of land owe their origin to this plough. It is mentioned in Co. Lit. 5a, that a bovate or oxgang is as much land as an ox can cultivate, and a plough-land as much as one plough can cultivate; and it was said that eight oxgangs make a plough-land (see Co. Lit. 69a).

Now a gebur, according to the *Rectitudines*, was to have his yard-land; and a yard, or *virgata terræ*, varied, according to Lord Coke (Co. Lit. 5a) from ten to twenty, twenty-five or thirty acres, on an average about one-fourth of the extent which a plough could cultivate in a year, and therefore about equal to two oxgangs. Hence the gebur could not afford to keep a plough of his own. Several, therefore, must unite in order to maintain a plough, and the gebur was, accordingly, to be supplied with two oxen, so that four geburs could have a plough among them, and employ it in cultivating the land which they held in severalty.

The fact that the land was thus cultivated in common by no means proves that it was owned in common. I can therefore see, in the circumstance of a common cultivation, no sufficient reason for holding that these intermixed fields were not, in numerous instances, the holdings of villeins which, in process of time, were converted into copyholds.

The second fact, that these intermixed fields were subject to a common right of pasture, after the crop had been removed, appears to be equally insufficient for the purpose of establishing Mr. Nasse's conclusion. Depasturing of cattle and sheep, upon small portions of uninclosed land, held by several occupiers, must be enjoyed, if at all, by them in common; and the exigencies of cultivation by a common plough forbade inclosures. It was for the general benefit that the stubble and other pasturage should not be wasted; and the fact of a common enjoyment by no means proves that the land itself was common property.

VI.

MR. SEEBOHM.

The preceding chapters, as well as nearly all the subsequent parts of this book, were written before Mr. Seebohm's work on *Village Communities* and the *English Manor* appeared, and I congratulate myself on the fact, that the opinions I have expressed in the foregoing chapters are verified by Mr. Seebohm's accurate and laborious researches. He has, besides, thrown much new light on the economy of the English Manor in the centuries succeeding the Conquest.

He has traced with minute and extended inquiry the mode in which the arable land of England was then cultivated—shown that the villeins ploughed the land in parallel strips a furlong in length, with a space or balk between adjacent strips—that the strips belonging to one villein, and forming with their appurtenances his virgate or yard of land, were scattered over the open fields,—that they were held not in common but separately, were indivisible, and descended from father to son by a species of customary entail.

I do not find, however, that Mr. Seebohm has attempted to answer the question, why the land was cultivated in these strips. The practice can scarcely have arisen through any requirement of tenure. The strips generally contained half an acre. Why was not the virgate of the peasant divided into allotments, say of ten acres each, situate in each of the three great fields, supposing the land to be cultivated on the three field system?

I venture to suggest that the answer may be found in a custom, traces of which may still be observed in Cambridgeshire, and which prevailed, I believe, in other parts of the country.

The land, by skilful management of the plough, was thrown into ridges rising gradually from the sides to the middle, and having deep furrows between the ridges. The traces of these ridges are still called "high backs."

Now the land was brought into this form, as it is supposed on very probable grounds, with a view to drainage, at a period when tile drainage did not exist. Such distance as might be found by experience most suitable for this purpose would, of course, be left between the deep furrows.

The term acre was probably applied to as much land as the Saxon team of eight oxen could plough in a day, and this was found to be two high backs of a furlong in length. This block of land, therefore, became the normal acre. The width of the one strip, including the furrow was about eleven yards, of the two, twenty-two yards, one-tenth of a furlong.

Mr. Eyton has pointed out that the acre was a lineal, as well as a superficial measure, and equal to four poles or twenty-two yards, the width of an acre when its sides were, according to usual custom, a furlong in length.

This remark may throw some further light on Edward the Confessor's dream, of which Mr. Seebohm has given an interesting account and explanation.

The division of the land into strips would also, no doubt, be convenient in determining the amount of labour due from each ox.

VII.

THE FIRST TAXATION OF LAND.—THE HIDE.

I HAVE already mentioned that the hide of land appears to have been the quantity held sufficient to support a freeman and his family. *Familia* in Bede is rendered *Hida*.[1] An estate consisting of a hide must have comprised a residence for the owner and the buildings required for the cultivation of the land. It is also clear, from numerous authorities, that a hide contained as much arable as a plough could conveniently cultivate in a year, the Saxons being familiar with the greatest of all the inventions which have been made in agriculture, the application of animal labour to the tillage of the soil. The hide contained also a small quantity of meadow, to provide hay for the oxen of the plough, and it comprised sufficient pasture for the cattle and sheep, which seem always to have formed an important adjunct in English husbandry. *Pastura ad pecuniam villæ*—pasture for the animals of the villa

---

[1] Bed. *Hist. Ecc.* 3, 24 ; 4, 13, 16, 19.

or manor—is the unfailing accompaniment of the arable land or *terra* registered in *Domesday*. There was also, in many cases, *pannage*, or feeding for the swine in the oak woods: the pastures and pannage by no means necessarily adjoining the arable.

The extent of the hide probably varied, in some degree, from one part of the country to another. Mr. Eyton, after a very careful examination, estimates the average hide in the county of Dorset at 240 acres. Now the virgate, or yard land, contained on an average about twenty-four acres, and was estimated, as I have mentioned, to be as much land as two oxen could plough in a year. The eight oxen of the Saxon plough would therefore suffice for about ninety-six acres. We may suppose, then, that the hide was originally divided, not very unequally, into arable and pasture, the latter tending to predominate. If an estate consisted of many hides, the same proportion of arable to pasture was probably preserved.

We may describe the original hide as an allotment containing arable for one plough, with the appropriate quantity of pasture and meadow.

The first taxation of land in England took place under Ethelred about the year 994, and the land was assessed by the hide. The reason for adopting this system is obvious. The assessors could readily ascertain how many ploughs were employed in cultivating each estate, and they appear to have usually assessed it accordingly.

It would be unnecessary in most instances to take the pasture into account, because its value might be assumed to be much less than that of the plough land, besides being generally proportionate to it in extent. If the estate did not contain an exact number of hides, the fractions were estimated in virgates and in acres; the virgate, no doubt, like the hide, comprising, not merely the arable, but the appurtenant right of pasture also. There were, as I have mentioned, four virgates of arable to the plough land, each virgate contributing two oxen to the plough. So there were to the hide four complete virgates, comprising arable land and rights of pasture. It is mentioned in the *Rectitudines* that the gebur was provided with six sheep and a cow as well as two oxen.

It was usual for the owner of land to hold a portion—generally about one-half—in hand, or *in dominio*, the remainder being occupied by the villeins, and cottagers with gardens and orchards. As a villein generally occupied a yard of land, we may conclude that there would be regularly two villeins to each hide of land. In such a case, each villein would contribute his two oxen to the plough, while the owner would provide the remaining four.

Some confusion has arisen from the hide being occasionally spoken of as equivalent to the plough-land—a mode of expression which was, I have no doubt, adopted, in consequence of the plough-land being the more valuable part of the hide, and the rest of the hide being regarded merely as an accessory to the plough-land or *carucata*.

Domesday gives the number of hides at which each property was assessed at the death of King Edward the Confessor, and at the date of the survey. It gives also the number of carucates or ploughlands, and these often exceed in number the number of hides. It would appear that the extent of land under the plough at the date of the original valuation had been subsequently increased; and the remark is sometimes added that one or two more carucates could be made.

After the hide had been taken as the unit of taxation, it came to signify a property which was rated at the value of an average hide; and, accordingly, as Mr. Eyton has shown, the assessment, in many instances, was not based entirely on the extent of the land assessed, but that advantages or disadvantages of situation were also taken into account. A hide at the date of the Domesday survey meant, therefore, land assessed at the value of an average ploughland with its appurtenances of pasture, &c.

VIII.

SAXON LAW OF SUCCESSION TO LAND.

THERE is not, as far as I am aware, any distinct authority respecting the law of succession to land of free tenure among the Anglo-Saxons, in case of intestacy.

It has been conjectured that the custom of Gavelkind, which still subsists in a large part of Kent, was once general throughout the kingdom.

The 71st and 79th laws of Cnut[1] are sometimes quoted in support of this opinion. Now the 71st law merely directs that the "aeht" shall be divided. This word signifies cattle and swine. That it does not include land appears from the 78th law, which provides that he who flees from the enemy shall forfeit land and aehtan.

It is true that the 79th law directs that, "if a man fall before his lord," then the heirs shall "shift" to the land and aehtan; but the loose and

[1] *Ancient Laws and Institutes of England*, edited by Thorpe, vol. i. pp. 412, 420.

general terms in which the law is expressed would be satisfied, by holding that the aeht are to be divided among the heirs of the movables, the next of kin, the land passing to the heir of the land, whoever he or they might be.

Neither is the theory, that equal succession among sons was the general rule, easily reconcilable with the fact that, in many towns and manors, the youngest son succeeded to the exclusion of his brothers. This custom still exists in a country inhabited by Saxons, in the northern part of Germany, Westphalia. I have before me a project of a law for regulating this course of descent. The custom was besides emphatically termed Borough English, showing that it must have existed in England before the Norman Conquest.

Again, on the vast manor of West Derby, the country between the Ribble and the Mersey (comprising many small manors) which belonged to Edward the Confessor, there were many free tenants, and the customs according to which they held their lands are recorded in *Domesday*. It is said, "Si quis terram patris mortui habere volebat XL. solidos relevabat: qui nolebat et terram et omnem pecuniam patris mortui rex habebat," *Domesday*, vol. ii., 269 b. —" If any one wished to have the land of his deceased father he paid 40s. relief," but there is no mention of more than one son succeeding. The holdings were apparently indivisible.

There can be little doubt that the manor, both of the Norman and Saxon days, was not simply a house where the landowner resided, or might reside, but a homestead as well, with the buildings necessary for storing agricultural produce.

The same remark will apply to the owner of a single hide of some 240 acres.

The villein also must have had accommodation for his two beasts of the plough and provisions during the winter, as well as a house or cottage for residence.

Each of these holdings, the manor, the hide, and the virgate, was an agricultural unit, which could not be actually divided without considerable difficulty.

At the present day, the owner of an estate will not readily divide a farm of ordinary extent, as he will hesitate, even if it be too large for a single tenant, in view of the expense which must be incurred in providing another farm-house and other farm-buildings. Now the ancient manor could not be divided without even greater difficulty than a modern farm, and the succession of several children, however equitable, would in numerous instances be highly inconvenient. The difficulty of actually dividing the land, might, it is true, be avoided by a sale and division of the proceeds: but in the times we are considering, few persons would have saved money enough to purchase any considerable property. In the absence of any other plausible theory to account for the prevalence in Kent of the custom which gave the land to all the sons equally, perhaps I may be permitted to conjecture that it may have proceeded from the superior wealth of this county, produced by the stream of foreign commerce which passed through it—from purchasers of land being readily found, and actual division therefore generally unnecessary.

I am disposed to think, therefore, that in Saxon times, actual division was the exception rather than the rule—that if there were sons, one would generally succeed to the exclusion of the others; the choice of the successor depending, partly on fitness to perform the duties attached to the land, partly on the will of the superior lord: and this opinion is, I think, confirmed, by the most ancient exposition of the English law of succession which we possess, and which is found in the treatise of Glanville; since from his statement it appears, that the rule of descent of non-military lands was, in his time, dependent on ancient custom.[1]

[1] Glanville, vii. 3.

IX.

EFFECT OF THE NORMAN CONQUEST ON THE DISTRIBUTION OF LAND.

THE statements contained in *Domesday Book* do not, I think, lead us to believe, that the Norman Conquest occasioned any very material effect on the magnitude of landed estates in England. The grants made to the immediate vassals of the Crown were, it is true, in many instances very extensive, but probably did not comprise more manors than were held by the Earls or Ealdormen and other great landowners previously to the battle of Hastings. Mr. Furley in his interesting and learned work on the Weald of Kent, vol. i., p. 233, points out that before the Conquest, there were in that county eleven immediate tenants of the Crown, and after the Conquest there remained the same number, notwithstanding the substitution of Normans for Saxons in the lay fees.

But whether the Norman tenants *in capite* held greater possessions than the Saxon magnates or not, there can be little doubt that the burdens imposed on the great estates were increased after the Conquest.

To insure the safety of the kingdom, for which such scant and unsystematic provision was made by the weak Saxon executive, castles were erected at important strategical points, such as Rochester, Tonbridge, Reigate, Bramber, Clare, &c., as well as on the borders towards Scotland and Wales; castles which became the residences and were probably built at the expense of the great feudal tenants, aided by forced labour; and were garrisoned by their retainers.

Not only was the defence of the kingdom strengthened, and its possession assured, by the erection of fortresses, but the grants made by the Crown were burdened by an obligation on the grantee to furnish, when called upon, a certain number of knights—that is, of armed horsemen, with sufficient attendants and provisions for forty days, during which they were bound to serve. According to the number of knights for whose service the grant was made, it was said to consist of so many knights' fees, and to be held by knight-service.

Those who received grants comprising many manors, retained some of the principal in their own hands, while the rest were granted by them to their followers, or remained in possession of the Saxon owners. These grants also were generally subject to the services of knights, proportionate in number to the magnitude of the grant. Some manors were estimated at several knights' fees, some at one knight's fee, and some at a portion of a fee. The Saxon proprietor who retained his land would probably not raise objections to the change of tenure as regarded military service, the principal difference between new and old being that he now held his property on condition of yielding such service to a subject, instead of directly to the state as formerly.

The burdens on landed property independent of military service were also increased. If the land descended to an infant heir, the lord was entitled to the profits during the minority of his tenant, while providing for his maintenance and education, and subject to the right of the widow to one-third of the land for her life. And the lord was also held entitled to dispose of the hand of his ward, whether male or female, in marriage, and to receive any amount which the relations of the other party to the match were willing to pay, in order to secure it. If the ward married without the lord's consent, the lord might obtain, out of the ward's property, the value of the marriage—the amount which it was estimated might have been secured by the lord as the price of his consent.

It seems probable, that these fruits of the feudal tenure were grasped with a strict and vigorous hand from the greater vassals alone. At least the great vassals do not appear to have considered, that the burdens to which they were subjected, received sufficient compensation, through their corresponding rights against those who held of themselves by military service. The establishment of the Court of Wards and Liveries, at the Reformation, must have rendered the collection of the feudal dues of the Crown, from the tenants *in capite*, more certain and rigorous than before.

We may therefore, I think, conclude that the feudal system, as it existed in England, did not favour the growth of the great estates, although the effect of the heavy burdens to which they were regularly subject, may have been, in some cases, compensated through the escheats and forfeitures by which they were occasionally augmented.

In some of the larger manors, there were probably tenants who held of the lord by military service—but this second sub-infeudation was, I think, rare. The socmen, though it may be, reduced in numbers, remained as tenants of the manor: they were, of course, still free, and still held by some certain service or payments in money or kind, and by the obligation or service of attending the manor court, at stated intervals. These courts do not seem to have been materially interfered with at the Conquest The possession of such a court continued to be held in estimation, as affording an accession of dignity, as well as a source of profit. And an estate, on which a court could not be held, either through want of free tenants, or absence of prescriptive right, was not considered worthy to be dignified with the name of Manor. In order that an estate might be entitled to the appellation, it must have "sac and soc," words which clearly indicate the Saxon origin of the jurisdiction. The court, however, obtained a Norman name—that of Court Baron—the court of the lord's men or free tenants.

I am not aware of any reason for supposing that the condition of the peasant class, the actual tillers of the soil, was affected in any sensible degree, by the introduction of feudalism. That system moved above their heads. To intrust serfs with arms was no more a part of the Norman, than of the Saxon constitution.

Among the current errors of political writers and speakers respecting the ancient tenures of land, there is none more common than to represent serfage as a feudal institution; although serfage has notoriously existed in Russia, Egypt, and other countries where feudalism was never established; and although, in countries which became feudal, the introduction of feudalism had been preceded for centuries by the custom of serfage. Serfage was, in fact, a purely agricultural, and feudalism a purely military institution.

X.

NORMAN LAW OF SUCCESSION.

WHATEVER may have been the general law of the country on the subject of succession to land in Saxon times, the rule that the eldest son should succeed to land held by military service, had speedily been settled after the Norman Conquest.

During at least the first century after the Conquest, feudalism in England was a reality. The vassal followed his lord in war. The relation between the two was so intimate, that it could not be dissolved without the consent of both. It originated in the act of homage, constituting a contract, by which the one expressly became the man of the other, of "life and limb and worldly honour;" and which carried with it an implied obligation, on the part of the lord, to protect his man. Hence the vassal could not alienate the land, which was the reward and retainer for his personal services, and enabled him to perform them, without his lord's approval.

The vassal might, however, make a sub-infeudation of part, at least, of his land, and the sub-vassal did not become the vassal of the superior lord; he did homage not to the superior lord, but to the vassal, by whom the land was granted to him. It was a maxim of feudal law, "*vassallus mei vassalli non est meus vassallus.*"

As the vassal could not transfer his land to another, without his lord's consent, so neither could the lord transfer his vassal's services to another, without the consent of the vassal.

It is not surprising that, when the relation between lord and vassal was thus strictly regulated, the right of giving lands by will, which was certainly permitted, as regards some freehold lands, by Saxon law, should have been lost with respect to land held by knight service. The vassal could not be permitted to replace his own services by those of a stranger, who might, possibly, be a personal enemy of the lord: and the reciprocal attachment of lord and vassal would also tend to give the descendants of the vassal an incontestable title to succession.

These considerations do not entirely explain the fact that, if the vassal left several sons, he was succeeded by the eldest alone.

That primogeniture was not a necessary consequence of feudalism, we find from one of the earliest treatises on feudal law, the first of the *Libri feudorum* (Titles I. and VIII.) generally annexed to the *Corpus Juris Civilis*, which expressly provides that, on the death of a vassal, the feud shall be divided equally among his sons.

With regard to the origin of primogeniture in England, it should not be forgotten that, as England received the feudal institutions from the Normans, so the Normans had previously adopted them in imitation of the French; who had established feudalism, throughout the greater part of France, in the latter half of the ninth century, not long before the permanent settlement of Normandy under Rollo. Now in France primogeniture has prevailed in the succession of feudal grants, and it is probable therefore, that in the history of that country there are to be found the main causes from which the custom proceeded, and it appears to have been adopted with other feudal institutions by the Normans from the French, and by the English after the Norman invasion, as a part of the body of laws which they accepted almost in its entirety.[1] In like manner, at rather a later period, Scotland voluntarily embraced feudalism in imitation of England, and also established the rule of primogeniture, and with slight modifications, the other English rules of succession to land.

The inconveniences always attending an actual division of the land would be enhanced, when it was

---

[1] We find that according to the *Établissements de l'Echiquier de Normandie* (Paris, 1839), p. 9, the eldest son succeeded to the "fief of the hauberk" to the exclusion of his brothers—but the date of this rule is uncertain.

held as a retainer for military services, because the services also would have to be apportioned; and we may conjecture that these difficulties assisted in establishing the custom, which gave to one son the land of his father; and, although the eldest might be by no means the fittest to fulfil the duties of a vassal, yet the advantage of having a fixed rule, the probability that when the father died in youth or middle age, the eldest son would be most capable of bearing arms, and the prestige which has always attended primogeniture seem to have been sufficient to recommend that rule in England, as in Normandy and in France, which favoured the eldest son, with respect to land held by knight service.

Two centuries after the Conquest we find the law of primogeniture applied to freehold lands, as well those held by socage as by military tenure, with scarcely any exception beyond the bounds of Kent, and certain boroughs, in which equal division and succession of the youngest prevailed respectively. The latter tenure also remained, as regarded the lands of villeins, in many manors, particularly in those of Sussex. Although, however, the actual division of land and services must have always been attended with difficulty, especially in early times, this inconvenience did not prevent, in England, the succession of daughters equally. The succession of females probably formed no part of the most ancient form of feudalism, but was introduced when the fee was ceasing to be a retainer, and becoming simply the property of the vassal, subject to certain financial rights of his lord; whilst at this time, the death of a vassal leaving male issue being an event much more usual, than the death of a vassal leaving only several daughters, the succession of the eldest son had been too firmly established, by custom, to be altered by considerations of equity, when the rule with regard to daughters was settled.

It appears, I think, from these considerations, that the introduction of the feudal system must have had a tendency to preserve large estates, by discouraging alienation *inter vivos*, forbidding alienation by will, and, in some instances, giving to one son lands which, by custom, might have been divisible among several.

Much interesting information on the subject of primogeniture may be found in two essays by C. S. Kenny and P. M. Laurence, Cambridge, 1878, which divided the Yorke prize.

XI.

STRICT ENTAILS—THE STATUTE "DE DONIS CONDITIONALIBUS."

No very remarkable change was made in laws directly affecting land in England, during the two centuries immediately succeeding the Norman Conquest. Magna Carta defined and regulated, without materially altering, the feudal tenure, and promised to freemen, without distinction, the protection of the law against arbitrary proceedings by the Crown. Nor were the villeins passed over with complete neglect; a clause, the 20th chapter of John's charter, provided that if the villein were amerced, his wainage should be saved. The Provisions of Merton, twenty years later than Magna Carta, empowered the owners of manors to appropriate a portion of their waste lands, provided that enough pasture was left for the use of their freehold tenants, but the statute is silent respecting the villeins, though now rising into copyholders.

Great changes however, were in course of preparation. During the long reign of Henry III. the country, on the whole, was prosperous, and increased in wealth. Notwithstanding the loud complaints respecting the exactions of Rome, stately cathedrals of exquisite beauty arose throughout England; and, in her social condition, a new order of men was in course of formation, destined to become a power in the state. Since the seat of the great court for determining private suits, Common Pleas, had been rendered stationary by Magna Carta, and had been established in the hall of the Palace at Westminster, many practitioners in that court had become learned in the customs of the realm, and, to a certain extent, acquainted with the laws of Rome. The *servientes ad legem* began to rival in credit the *servientes ad arma*. The tendency to place greater reliance upon law, and to favour those who were engaged in administering it, became manifest in England, and, we may add, about the same time, in France also.

It was in the year 1285, the 13th of Edward I. that the famous statute *De Donis Conditionalibus*, which gave to all owners of freehold land in England, the power of strictly entailing it, was passed. It was by no means a solitary enactment like Magna Carta, or the Provisions of Merton, but formed part of the great body of remedial laws passed in the reign of Edward I., which obtained for himself the not wholly inappropriate designation of the English Justinian. No one, I think, can peruse this body of legislation, without being convinced that it was the work of men well versed in the laws as they then existed :—not the result of a sudden effort, but of continuous labour and mature deliberation, and that these laws had for their authors the learned serjeants of Westminster Hall.

There is a class of writers on law, especially on laws relating to land, who attribute various legislative acts to profound political designs, now of the nobles, now of the sovereign; and accordingly allege that the statute *De Donis* was the work of the nobility, intent on increasing the power of their order. But even without recalling the just maxim of Napoleon, that in politics the present alone is regarded, the notion that the law of entail was framed by the peers, with such a political purpose as I have mentioned, is singularly wanting in probability. The barons had not only been discredited, by the failure of their attempt to govern the country, by means of a ministry or committee selected by themselves from their own order, but their power had been crushed, for the time, by Prince Edward at Evesham, where their great military and political leader Simon de Montfort was slain. On the demise of Henry III. seven years afterwards, Prince Edward, a cautious man, felt his power so assured, that he did not hasten to England in order to take possession of the Crown, but spent two years in Italy and France, on his homeward journey from the Holy Land. After his return, and before the thirteenth year of his reign, when the statute *De Donis* was passed, he had subdued Llewellyn, and permanently annexed North Wales to the English Crown. Yet it was by this monarch and at this time, according to the opinion I have mentioned, that the statute *De Donis* was passed at the instance of the nobility, in order to depress the power of the Crown; and we are asked to believe that the King, a man of wide experience and undoubted sagacity, was outwitted or overawed by an illiterate and disheartened body of barons.

If we look at the preamble of the statute, and the preamble of a statute is generally the best key to the intention of its authors, we shall see it stated that their object was to prevent what must, I think, be admitted to have been a grievance.

Suppose that a man, on the marriage of his daughter, gave a portion of his land to her husband and the heirs of his body by the wife. Then if the wife had issue, the husband might as the law stood before the statute was passed, alienate the land leaving the issue unprovided for.

If no alienation took place, the land on the death of the donee would descend to the issue of the marriage like an ordinary estate in fee simple. But, if the donee died without leaving issue, or if, after his decease, his issue failed, and the land had not been alienated, the donor or his heir would have the land again.

If, on the other hand, after issue born the donee alienated the land, he, as we have seen, disinherited his heirs, and also deprived the donor of his chance of reversion. This as the statute says, "to the giver seemeth hard," and it therefore enacted that, for the future, the will of the giver should be observed according to the form of the gift, and that they, to whom the land was given, should have no power to alienate it. It seems to me that the hardship thus referred to in the preamble of the statute *De Donis*, was sufficiently real to account for its enactment, without attributing any deep political designs to its authors.

XII.

EFFECTS OF STRICT ENTAILS.

The evils arising from strict entails, vividly depicted by modern writers, appear to have escaped the observation of contemporaries. They do not allege that agriculture retrograded, or that the condition of the rural population deteriorated, under the operation of the statute *De Donis*.

It was during the period in which the statute was in full force, that, in the great forest of the Weald (according to Mr. Furley, the historian of the Weald of Kent) extensive clearings were made, and an industrious agricultural population took the place of the herds of swine which, from the most remote ages, had been the principal inhabitants.

Serfdom was rapidly disappearing before the advance of wealth and prosperity. The labourers began to claim freedom as a right, and strove, not always without success, to break the antiquated links, which still bound some of their number to the soil.

With reference to the general state of England in the fourteenth century, during the whole of which the statute *De Donis* remained in almost entirely unimpaired force, Lord Macaulay says :—

"Every yeoman from Kent to Northumberland valued himself as one of a race born to victory and dominion, and looked down with scorn on the nation before which his ancestors had trembled. . . . France had no infantry that could face the English bows and bills. . . . Nor were the arts of peace neglected by our fathers during this stirring period. While France was wasted by war, until she at length found in her own desolation a miserable defence against invaders, the English gathered in their harvests, adorned their cities, pleaded, traded, and studied in security."—Macaulay's *History of England*, i. p. 18.

The effects of the statute *De Donis* upon the distribution of land, have, I think, been greatly exaggerated. That very large estates existed in England long before the statute was passed has, in the preceding pages, been abundantly demonstrated. Its effects in preventing division have been dwelt upon, whilst its operation in checking accumulation has been almost wholly overlooked. The main causes of accumulation in ancient, as in modern times, will be found in the marriage of heirs with heiresses, and the investment in land of fortunes amassed by commerce : the mere landowner, whether his estate was entailed or not, being rarely in a condition to become a purchaser.

Now the statute in many instances opposed an effectual bar to accumulation by either of these modes. If land on being entailed were given, as it often, perhaps generally, was given, to a man and the heirs male of his body, it could not pass, so long as a male descendant existed, to any female, and so long therefore, the union by marriage of such an estate with another also entailed on male issue became, while such issue survived, impossible. Just as two kingdoms, in which the Salic Law prevails, can never become consolidated by marriage. In the same way the rich citizen of London, of Hull, or Bristol, bent upon purchasing land enough for the founder of a county family, must often have been checked in the attempt, by coming upon some Naboth's vineyard, protected from annexation by the statute *De Donis*.

For the origin of large estate we must therefore, as has already been shown, look to a period long anterior to this statute.

That the statute did produce evils and inconveniences cannot be doubted, since, otherwise, the judges of the Common Pleas would not have sanctioned the transparent collusion, by which the heir in tail was deprived of his legal right. What these evils and inconveniences were, we may learn from Lord Coke, whose statements rest upon recorded facts, and not like the assertions of many modern writers, on preconceived opinions.

Lord Coke observes, "When all estates were fee simple, then were purchasers sure of their purchases, farmers of their leases, creditors of their debts, the king and lords had their escheats, forfeitures, wardships and other profits of their seignories: and for this and other like cases, by the wisdom of the Common Law, all estates of inheritance were fee simple; and what contentions and mischiefs have crept into the quiet of the law by these fettered inheritances, daily experience teaches us."— *Co. Lit.* 19b.

The danger to purchasers with which Lord Coke heads his indictment against entails, appears to have arisen in manner such as this. The descent even of an unentailed estate from father to son, for some generations, was, in his day, of no rare occurrence. The purchaser of an estate which had so descended, might believe that he was buying a fee simple, while in fact, an ancient deed entailing the land in the course of descent, which had already taken place, had been executed and forgotten. On the existence of the deed being discovered, the heir in tail of the vendor might insist, that in compliance with the statute, the will of the donors "according to the form of the gift," should be observed, and the purchaser would be without remedy, except perhaps under a clause of "warranty." Creditors by securities binding the heir might be defeated in the same manner, and the Crown and other lords might be disappointed, in rare cases, of forfeiture and escheats for treason or felony.

That these were the real evils which arose from the statute, and that it did not produce the pernicious consequences either to the nobility, the esquires or the other freeholders of England which are frequently attributed to it, we have thus given reason to believe by the testimony of Lord Coke and Lord Macaulay.

Scotland had no statute corresponding to our statute *De Donis*, but attempts were made in that country to establish strict entails by clauses of "irritancy and resolution," purporting to make void alienation, but the validity of such clauses had by no means been admitted before the act of 1685, c. 22, which expressly recognises their authority, and the absolute right of heirs to succeed according to the disposition of the entailer, *Erskine Inst.*, Book iii. Tit. viii. 25, and this law with no very important modifications remained in force until 1848, when by 11 and 12 Vic., c. 36 § 1, tenant in tail in possession was empowered to acquire the fee simple, if born after the deed of entail was executed, at his own discretion, or if born before the execution, with the consent of the next heir of entail.

It is worthy of note, that the period during which the law permitted the establishment of strict entails in Scotland, coincides with that during which Scottish agriculture underwent the greatest improvements.

XIII.

RELAXATION OF STRICT ENTAILS—COMMON RECOVERIES.

I HAVE already stated that the statute *De Donis* remained in nearly unimpaired force during the fourteenth century. Even if the owner of entailed land sold it, with a warranty that he held in fee simple, his heir in tail might claim the land by force of the entail, notwithstanding that the obligation of the warranty would, according to the ordinary rules of law, by descending upon him, preclude him from asserting his right. This was the case of a lineal warranty; but if the warranty were collateral, if the warranty did not, and could not, descend from or through the ancestor from whom the entailed land descended, then the heir in tail was barred.

The cases in which a collateral warranty existed must, however, have been rare, and owners of entailed lands, with the view of obtaining complete control over them, had recourse to this expedient. The owner instructed a friend to bring an action against himself, in due form, in the Court of Common Pleas, seeking that the right to the land might be adjudged to the complainant. Simply to have allowed judgment to go by default, a mere *cessio in jure,* would not have bound the heir of the owner. The owner therefore alleged that some other person had warranted the title of the land to him (the owner), and that person was admitted to defend the action in place of the owner, according to the usual course of law, as the person on whom the loss would ultimately fall, if the plaintiff succeeded in his suit. At the hearing the alleged warrantor made default, and judgment was given that the plaintiff should recover the land in dispute, and the original defendant should have an equivalent out of the lands of the warrantor.

If the defendant in the collusive action died, and his heir brought his action founded on the gift in tail, he was met by the objection, that his ancestor had received an equivalent for the land entailed, which equivalent must have descended to the present claimant, as heir to his ancestor.

It is most probable that this decision first took place in a hostile suit, in which the heir in tail was really in possession of the equivalent; and that some astute lawyer, seeing that the court assumed, without proof, that the heir had inherited the equivalent for which his ancestor had obtained judgment, perceived that a door was open for escaping from the trammels of an entail, by means of a pretended warranty and judgment thereupon.

Taltarum's Case, decided by the Court of Common Pleas, in the 12 Ed. IV., 1472, is considered to have established the efficiency of such a proceeding in barring an estate tail against the heir. The language of the pleadings,[1] however, leads me to believe that the experiment was not a novel one, and that the defendant, claiming under the entail, relied on some facts which distinguished his case from the simple one I have described, rather than on the fact of the recovery being feigned and collusive.

As, however, this latter defence was raised by the pleadings, the judgment in favour of the plaintiff showed that the defence was untenable, and thus established the validity of a recovery of entailed land, where the ancestor of the plaintiff had also obtained a judgment for recovery of an equivalent against a warrantor, notwithstanding that the whole proceeding was notoriously feigned and collusive. It is probable that the Court was influenced, among other considerations, by the fear of shaking titles, which depended on admitting the validity of such recoveries.

The Court was also in all probability willing to favour a proceeding for converting an estate tail into an estate in fee simple, for the sake of diminishing the evils which were attendant on the former, and

---

[1] See Digby's *History of the Law of Real Property*, p. 220, for a translation of the pleadings.

were afterwards pointed out by Lord Coke, as I have already mentioned.

A purchaser for a valuable consideration is said to be a favourite in a Court of Equity: he is in fact a favourite in every Court of Justice. That a man, who has given convincing proof of his good faith by paying his money, in order to obtain some stipulated advantage, has a strong claim to be protected in his purchases is unquestionable, and every court would lean in his favour, when the contest lies between him and a person claiming under an ancient gift, of which the purchaser has had no notice.

I do not, however, discover any ground, for attributing to the judges of the Common Pleas, the opinions expressed by modern writers, with regard to the injurious effects of entails on the cultivation of the soil, and the well-being of the people.

XIV.

HENRY VII. AND HIS NOBLES—THE STATUTE OF FINES.

The Statute of Fines, 4 Henry VII., c. 24 (1487), was made about fifteen years after Taltarum's case had established the right of the tenant in possession of entailed land to dispose of it absolutely.

This statute has afforded occasion of comment to those who discover deep political designs in the authors of every change in the law relating to land.

They allege that Henry VII., being a politic and sagacious prince, obtained the enactment with the view of depressing the power of his nobility; although the objections to such a theory are neither few nor inconsiderable.

The first objection is that the statute was really not the work of Henry VII. or his advisers, but of his predecessor Richard III., a prince whose hands were too full of pressing business, during his short reign, to leave him leisure for plans which could ripen, if at all, only in the distant future. The statute of Henry VII. differs in no essential particular from that of 1 Richard III., c. 7. The statute of Henry VII. merely relaxes the provisions for ensuring the publicity of a fine contained in the earlier statute.

There is another objection scarcely less fatal than the last to the assumption of a deep political design in the framers of the statute, that the design, if it existed, was so clumsily carried into effect by the words of the statute, that it became necessary about fifty years afterwards to pass another statute, the 32 Henry VIII., c. 36 (1540), to declare that the 4 Henry VII. applied to entailed estates at all. The 4th of Henry VII. was a general statute intended to restore (with modifications) the ancient rule of law, which made a fine or compromise of a suit concerning land in the King's Court, a bar to the suit of any one who did not claim the land comprised in the fine, within a certain period after the fine taking place. There was a saving clause in the statute of Henry VII., and most persons now reading it would, I think, conclude that the right of an heir in tail was within the saving clause, and therefore not intended to be affected by the general enactment.

There is also the third objection, that the law had already admitted the right of the tenant in tail in possession to acquire an absolute right to his land, by means of a common recovery, and further, that the common recovery was more effectual than the fine, because the former barred not merely the issue in tail, but all subsequent estates also, including that of the reversioner; whilst the Statute of Fines, 4 Henry VII., even after it had been explained by the statute of Henry VIII., barred the issue only, and left claimants whose estates were to take effect, after failure of issue of the tenant in tail, to assert their rights whenever they might accrue. It is true that a fine might be resorted to by tenant in tail in remainder, whilst a recovery could be effectively suffered by tenant in tail in possession only.

XV.

STRICT SETTLEMENTS.

THE decision of the Court of Common Pleas in the year 1472, established, as I have pointed out, that any person entitled to the possession of entailed land could become, at his pleasure, the absolute owner, by means of a friendly suit. The decision applied no less to the lands of peers than to those of commoners. Indeed, notwithstanding the rooted popular belief that estates of peers are, in some manner, connected with their titles, in order that their dignity may be maintained, the law has recognised no such distinction. Where, however, the reversion of landed property after the extinction of issue on whom the land was entailed, belonged to the Crown, the entail could not be barred by a common recovery, 34 & 35 Hen. VIII. c. 20, s. 2. Estates so circumstanced were and are not numerous; and as to the great mass of landed property in England, the power of strictly entailing it, conferred by the Statute de Donis, ceased in the fifteenth century, and has never since been revived. A few estates given for eminent public services, such as Woodstock and Strathfieldsaye, have, it is true, been strictly entailed, but this has been effected by special Acts of Parliament, in contravention of the general law of the land.

Soon after strict entails had thus been virtually abolished, the practice of settling lands, for the limited period which the rules of law permitted, was introduced. The owner of an estate desirous, for example, of making provision, on his son's marriage, for the son and his family, instead of granting the land to the son and the heirs male of the son's body, would give it to the son for his life only, in order to obviate the possibility of the son obtaining the power, through a recovery, of alienating the land absolutely. And the donor would provide by the settlement that, after the son's decease, the land should go to the son's eldest son and the heirs of his body. And in case of failure of the eldest son's issue, that the land should pass to the second son and the heirs of his body, with similar provisions for other sons according to seniority, or in any other order, and with any omissions which the settler might think proper to make. The security obtained by such a settlement that the land would long remain in the same family, fell far short of that which could be gained before the validity of recoveries to bar an estate tail had been established ; for if the son to whom the first estate in tail had been given (generally, of course, the eldest) attained twenty-one, then with the consent of his father, or of his own authority supposing the father to have died, a recovery might be suffered, the estate sold, and the other subsequent interests given by the settlement entirely defeated. As a son is usually born within three or four years after a marriage, a settlement on marriage generally becomes liable to be set aside within some five-and-twenty years after its execution. In the rare case of the eldest son marrying and dying in infancy, and leaving an infant heir, the liability would, no doubt, be deferred till that heir attained twenty-one. Marriage settlements of land have remained subject to the liabilities I have mentioned ever since their introduction, and so remain at the present day.

We sometimes hear it said that the "law of settlement" should be abolished, as if there were some law in existence which favoured settlements of land. No such law can, however, be pointed out, although there are rules of law, by which the power of making settlements is restrained within the narrow limits which I have mentioned, and which will be more fully stated below.

It cannot have been long after the liability of estates tail to alienation had been established, when settlements, nearly in the form I have explained and now in use, were introduced. The settlement, the provisions of which were the subject of litigation in Chudleigh's case (1 Co. Rep. 113) was made in the 3rd and 4th Ph. and Mary (1556), and contained limitations of the nature I have explained, and there is no reason for holding that this was by any means the first settlement of the kind. A little research would, I believe, bring earlier instances to light. Settlements of land such as I have described, strict settlements as they are called, possessed manifest advantages over the grants of estates tail which they had superseded. No provision for younger children was compatible with the estate tail, unless we admit that the right of a widow to dower, the right, that is, to one-third of the land for her life, frequently, no doubt, applied to their support, could be so considered. In addition to provision for younger children a settlement can be moulded entirely at the pleasure of the settler; it may prefer a younger son to an elder, a daughter to a son, it may give to younger children any part or the whole of the estate. In short, the law, in accordance with the genius of the English people, leaves the settler absolutely unfettered with regard to the disposition of his property; restraining him only by forbidding provisions, which would give an interest in the property to an unborn person, if that person would not necessarily take the interest during the life of a person in existence at the time of the settlement, or within a period of twenty-one years and a few months from the death of such person. This is "the rule against perpetuities" to which the Courts have strictly adhered, and which applies equally to land and to personal property. The ordinary strict settlement of land, as will be seen from the example I have given, by no means takes advantage of the utmost limits of the law.

XVI.

EFFECT OF STRICT SETTLEMENTS OF LAND—
MR. THOROLD ROGERS.

IN a valuable work on agriculture and prices in the middle ages, the following impassioned and eloquent passage occurs:—"No English labourer in his most sanguine dreams has the vista of occupying, still less of possessing, land. He cannot rise in his calling. He cannot cherish any ambition, and he is, in consequence, dull and brutish, reckless and stupid.

"We owe the fact that the great English nation is tenant at will to a few thousand landowners to that device of evil times, a strict settlement. We are informed that the machinery which has gradually changed the whole character of the rural population of England, was invented by the subtlety of two lawyers of the Restoration, Palmer and Bridgman. As there have been men whose genius has bestowed lasting benefits on mankind, so there have been, from time to time, exhibitions of perverse intellectual activity, whose malignant influence has inflicted permanent evils. It may be that the mischief is too widespread for remedial measures. But no Englishman who has the courage to forecast the destinies of his country can doubt that its greatest danger lies in the present alienation of the people from the soil, and in the future exodus of a discontented peasantry."[1]

Although well accustomed to the somewhat exaggerated terms which often characterise attacks on the English law of real property, I had considerable difficulty in discovering the particular mischief floating in the mind of the author, against which the above pathetic passage was directed.

It is well known that strict settlements of land were, as I have shown above, introduced more than a century before the Restoration, and could not, therefore, have been, as supposed by the writer, the invention of lawyers of that period; and as the evil results which moved his indignation manifested themselves, according to his statement, only through the malignant influence of such lawyers, it cannot be supposed that strict settlements produced these evils. As to the mode in which strict settlements prevented the labourer from obtaining land (the effect which the author attributes to them), he is entirely silent. He simply assumes the fact. Does he wish it to be understood that the labourer could

[1] *History of Agriculture and Prices in England*, by James E. Thorold Rogers, M.A. Oxford, vol. i. p. 693.

not obtain land, because there was no land in the market in consequence of the introduction of settlements? But settlements still exist, and yet it is notorious that abundance of land is always to be purchased, at a price which does not exceed what may be called the natural level, the price of Government securities yielding the same annual income. Nor can it, I believe, be shown that it was formerly more difficult to purchase land than it is at present. The delusion that "the English nation is tenant at will to a few thousand landowners" was dispelled by Lord Derby's *Domesday Book*, showing that their number is about a million.

The key to the passage I have quoted will, I think, be found in the second volume of Blackstone's *Commentaries*, p. 165, in Kerr, third edition.

Speaking of strict settlements of land in the form which they first assumed, Blackstone says: "In these cases, therefore, it was necessary to have trustees appointed to preserve the contingent remainders" (the estates granted to the first and other sons in the example I have given), "in whom there was vested an estate in remainder for the life of the tenant for life, to commence when his estate determined. If, therefore, his estate for life determined otherwise than by his death, the estate of the trustees for the term of his natural life took effect, and became a particular estate in possession, sufficient to support the remainders depending in contingency.

This method is said to have been invented by Sir Orlando Bridgman, Sir Geoffrey Palmer, and other eminent counsel, who betook themselves to conveyancing during the time of the civil wars, in order to secure in family settlements a provision for the future children of an intended marriage, who, before, were usually left to the mercy of a particular tenant for life; and when, after the Restoration, those gentlemen came to fill the first offices of the law, they supported their invention within reasonable and proper bounds, and introduced it into general use."

It appears, therefore, that Bridgman and Palmer merely introduced a clause into some strict settlements, making them somewhat more strict than they otherwise would have been, and that these perversely intellectual lawyers were far removed from being the inventors of strict settlements.

I propose to consider in the next chapter whether the invention of trustees to preserve contingent remainders can have produced the disastrous effects attributed to the perverse ingenuity of Palmer and Bridgman by Professor Rogers.

XVII.

TRUSTEES TO PRESERVE CONTINGENT REMAINDERS.

EVERY one conversant with the working of settlements is aware, that the introduction of trustees to preserve contingent remainders can have had any effect in rare and exceptional instances only. But the vast importance attached by so able and learned a writer as Mr. Rogers to the change in the practice of conveyances, which took place at the Restoration, makes it desirable, that the nature of this change and the extent of its operation should be clearly and explicitly stated.

When land was given to one for life, with remainder after his decease to his sons and their issue successively in the usual form, the interests given to the sons were, previously to the birth of a son, said to be contingent, because they could have no immediate effect, in consequence of there then being no one to take them. In such circumstances it was possible, that the father, who had the life interest, might acquire, by purchase or descent, the absolute reversionary right to the land, or reversion in fee simple, as it is termed, expectant on the determination or failure of the intermediate interests given to his children and the heirs of their bodies. In such a case, if no son had been born or was living, there would be no actual or vested interest, no interest which had an existing owner, intervening between the life interest given by the settlement and the ultimate reversion afterwards acquired by the owner of the life interest. And it is a rule of law, adopted with a view to simplification, that if the same person has two interests in the same land, one to commence when the other terminates, and the second in time is of a nature as high as the first or superior to it, then the two will coalesce, the first being merged or drowned in the second, the commencement of which will of course be accelerated. The unborn children of a marriage, upon the celebration of which a strict settlement of land had been made, were therefore liable to be deprived of the benefit intended for them, if no issue entitled under the settlement were in existence, and the husband, the tenant for life, acquired the ultimate property, the reversion or remainder in fee of the land, when the life estate would be merged in the fee; and although a child might afterwards come into existence, who would have been entitled to an intermediate interest under the settlement if no merger had taken place, the law would not undo, on his account, what it had already done, but would treat the interest of the child as non-existent. This is the main, if not the only chance of a settled estate becoming alienable, which is guarded against by the invention of Palmer and Bridgman.

Now in the first place the cases would be few in which the husband could acquire, before there was a son issue of the marriage, the remainder expectant on the determination of the provision for his children and their descendants; and the cases must have been fewer still in which an English gentleman, while any hope of issue remained, would take advantage of a legal technicality, for the sake of depriving his own progeny of the benefits provided for them by a solemn compact to which he had, as was usually the case, been himself a party, or under which, if not a party to it, he had taken a substantial benefit.

But not only did these difficulties stand in the way of defeating a strict settlement, but the danger of its being thus set aside might be guarded against, even before the days of Bridgman and Palmer, by placing the property in the hands of trustees. To suppose, therefore, that the introduction of a device to prevent contingent remainders from the danger of being thus defeated—a danger which, as we have seen, could exist in rare instances only—produced the deterioration in the position of the English labourer alleged to have taken place by Mr. Rogers, appears to me a conclusion for which even a show of probability is entirely wanting; and that if the English labourer has indeed, since the Restoration, as Professor Rogers asserts, become "brutish, reckless, and stupid,"—an assertion, however, which I venture to controvert—the cause must be sought elsewhere than in the invention of strict settlements of land, or of trustees to preserve contingent remainders.

XVIII.

POWERS OF SALE.

The invention of trustees to preserve contingent remainders was followed by the introduction into settlements of provisions, which enabled trustees to sell the estate (subject generally to the consent of the tenant for life), and to invest the moneys arising from the sale in the purchase of other lands, to be settled with limitations the same as those with which the estate sold had been settled. Such powers were found convenient, especially where some circumstance had occurred rendering a settled estate less eligible for residence, or had increased its value as a site for building. These powers, however, occasionally favoured accumulation. Before they were employed, the settlement of an estate offered a barrier, for some time at least, against its annexation to a neighbouring property, although, of course, not so durable a barrier as a strict entail. If settled estates could be sold under a power, a rich neighbour, by a tempting offer, might induce the trustees to sell, with the view of investing the purchase-money in another property producing perhaps a larger income.

The legislature has by various statutes, and particularly by Lord Cairns's Act (Settled Lands Act, 1882), 45 and 46 Vic. c. 38, much increased the facility for selling settled estates. The tenant for life can now himself, without the consent of trustees, absolutely dispose of the property, with the exception of the principal mansion and its demesne, which cannot be sold without the consent of the trustees of the settlement, or order of the court. It is provided that the moneys to arise from a sale of settled land shall be paid into court, or to the trustees of the settlement, and invested in land, government stock, or other securities in which trustees are authorised to invest moneys, or railway debentures, upon the trusts and provisions of the settlement.

Provision is made for the application of capital moneys arising from the sale of part of the settled lands in improvements sanctioned by the Land Commissioners; and the tenant for life is empowered to grant agricultural leases for twenty-one years, mining leases for sixty, and building leases for ninety-nine years.

An objection often urged against settlements of land, that a settled estate cannot be dealt with advantageously, through the interest of the possessor being limited in duration, appears to be entirely removed by these provisions, and it is difficult to see how they could be extended, without abolishing settlements of land altogether, and forbidding landowners to exercise the right of being prudent and making provision for their families—a right which is conceded to all other classes of society.

XIX.

INCLOSURE OF WASTE LANDS.—MR. JOHN WALTER—FORMATION OF A PEASANT PROPRIETARY.

A NOT inconsiderable alteration in the distribution of land in England took place at the end of the last and commencement of the present century, through the operation of inclosures. Under the sanction of Parliament, waste lands were divided among those who had rights of common over them, in proportion to the estimated value of those rights, and the area of cultivated land was thus considerably increased.

Some interesting statistics respecting inclosures are given in a pamphlet, entitled "*A Letter to the Electors of Berkshire*, by John Walter, Esq., 1839," from which it appears that, while the average number of Inclosure Acts from 1783 to 1793 was about thirty annually, the annual average rose to ninety from 1793 to the close of the war in 1815.

The inclosure of waste lands does not appear to have produced the improvement in the condition of the agricultural labourers which some economists expected as the consequence of the measure. On the contrary, as Mr. Walter states on the authority of Parliamentary Returns, the amounts annually expended on the relief of the poor rose from about two millions sterling in 1793, to four millions in 1803, and more than six millions at the end of the war in 1815.

The conclusion drawn by Mr. Walter from these statistics, that the inclosure of waste lands was injurious to the poorer commoners, is confirmed by the instance of at least one proposed inclosure, that of Bucklebury, by figures which show that a cottager benefited from uninclosed common land, in the article of fuel, to the value of 2*l*. 12*s*. annually, and in pasturage of a cow and other advantages, to the amount of more than 8*l*. a year; while the value of the allotment, which he was to receive in exchange, amounted to 2*l*. per annum only. It is not surprising that, with these facts before them, the House of Commons threw out the Bucklebury Inclosure Bill.

It is, however, plain that a large part of the increase in the amount expended on the poor is attributable to the same cause as that which occasioned the increase in inclosures, namely, the advance in the price of wheat which took place during the war. The poor-rates were swelled because wheaten bread entered largely into the consumption of the poor, and the high price of wheat stimulated inclosure, because when wheat was at from 50s. to 100s. and upwards a quarter, it could be cultivated with profit even on inferior lands.

It may well be doubted, however, whether this conversion of pasturage into tillage has been of permanent advantage to the country, and whether, independently of the interests of the poor, it would not have been well that the wastes should have remained in their original condition of pasture land.

One of the disadvantages attending inclosures was, according to Mr. Walter, that the recipients of small allotments were sometimes obliged to sell them, in order to meet their quotas of the expense attendant on procuring the Act. And this brings us in face of the great difficulty which besets small proprietors of land. Bad seasons inevitably come, when the produce is insufficient for the maintenance of the owner. He is compelled to seek an advance on the security of his land, and obtains it, not infrequently, on exorbitant terms. Favourable seasons seldom enable him to do more than pay the interest on the debt he has contracted; and one, two, or three successive bad harvests may produce foreclosure and ruin. The same cry comes from the Ganges and the Nile; the ryot and the fellah are in the grasp of the usurer. Legislation may mitigate, but cannot extirpate, the evil: for it lies in the very nature of things.

Even the French peasantry, economical as they are and inured to hardship, suffer grievously from the same cause: its effects in their case being, no doubt exaggerated by the law of succession, which tends to the perpetual subdivision of the land, and throws ever-increasing difficulties in the way of profitable cultivation. Meanwhile, agriculture in France shows little, if any, sign of improvement, there is no emigration, and yet the population, if not diminishing, is almost stationary.

The difficulties, which beset schemes for the establishment of permanent peasant proprietors, render it desirable to consider attentively those measures which have been found, in practice, beneficial to the agricultural labourers.

Experience has shown that small allotments, let at moderate rents, can be cultivated by agricultural labourers with advantage to themselves, and without interfering materially with their ordinary vocation. If this system were generally adopted, and in exceptionally bad years, attended with a reduction or remission of rent, the condition of the labourer would be raised, and the owner or farmer of the land would probably find, that the sacrifices, which he might occasionally be called upon to make, would be compensated, by a reduction of poor-rates, and an improvement in the moral qualities of his labourers.

This plan might be supplemented on considerable estates, by the formation of small farms, for the occupation of the labourers who showed most intelligence and energy in the cultivation of their allotments. Their rise in the social scale might be slow, but it would probably be more lasting than the sudden elevation of a labourer converted, without previous preparation, into a proprietor, who would be exposed to the strong temptation of mortgaging or selling his land.

PART II.

I.

AMENDMENT OF LAW OF PRIMOGENITURE.

It will be evident, I think, from the preceding statements, that the English "Land Laws" are not justly chargeable with the faults usually urged against them by advanced politicians, whose opinions upon the subject appear to be grounded, for the most part, on hasty assumptions. It cannot however be denied, that, in two respects at least, the English system of land tenure loudly demands amendment.

The Law of Primogeniture, although it operates but rarely, contravenes, in many instances, the wish of an intestate. The owner of a landed estate is, no doubt, usually desirous that it shall continue in his name and family. This may be condemned as a weakness by philosophers; but, like the desire of posthumous fame, it is frequently attended with beneficial results. Now, the owner, although opposed to the sale or division of his real estate, would, for the most part, deprecate no less strongly than sale or division, the exclusion of all members of his family except an eldest son, from any interest in his freehold property. In old times the widow could not be deprived of her dower, a life interest in one-third of the lands, held in fee-simple or fee-tail, of her husband, without her own consent, and the cumbrous procedure in the Court of Common Pleas called a fine; but as this state of the law was found inconvenient, in case it became desirable to sell the land during the joint lives of the husband and wife, conveyancers introduced a provision into purchase deeds, which had the effect of depriving the wife of her right to dower out of the purchased land; and they appear to have continued a similar practice, although the Dower Act of 1834 rendered it wholly unnecessary, because the sale of the land by the husband was, by virtue of the Act, sufficient to displace the right of the wife; and thus the provision which the law made for the widow, and which, of course, often became a temporary provision for younger children also, was needlessly swept away. So that, on an intestacy taking place, the eldest son generally excludes, not only the other children, but the widow also, from all interest whatever in the freehold property of his father, if the father has been the purchaser; although if he has inherited it, only the younger children are entirely excluded.

The present state of things is, therefore, even more objectionable than that which existed under the feudal law, when, as I have before mentioned, the third part of the land, which the widow enjoyed for her life, often must have afforded some support for younger children, as well as for herself.

It has often been pointed out as an excellence of the Statute for the Distribution of Intestates' Estates, that it makes for an intestate such a disposition of his personal property, as, in ordinary cases, a reasonable man would make for himself. Does it transcend the wisdom of Parliament to do the like with regard to freehold property? Why should it not preserve the right of the eldest son to take the land as heir to his father, and, at the same time, charge the land with a sum of money to be divisible, like the personal estate of the father, between the widow and the younger children or their issue; the proportion of the amount so distributable to the value of the land, varying according to the number of claimants? Such a law would give the eldest son a fair opportunity of retaining the land, without doing manifest injustice to other members of the family. It would remove a palpable grievance, with as little alteration as possible in the existing law, while avoiding the risk of encountering the evils which result from the constant subdivision of land.

II.

PROPOSED SYSTEM OF REGISTRATION.

There is another improvement in our land system which is much more urgently required than the amendment of the Law of Primogeniture. I refer to the establishment of Registers of deeds and wills relating to land.

The efforts of the legislature in this direction have been singularly unsuccessful—more unsuccessful, perhaps, than its other attempts to improve the laws relating to land.

Registers were established in the earlier part of the last century for Yorkshire and Middlesex, and two Acts for introducing a General Register have been passed in the present reign. The earlier attempts produced but slight advantage through doing too little, the later still slighter through endeavouring to do too much.

It is essential to a good system of registration that an intending purchaser or mortgagee should be able to ascertain, from an inspection of the register, what documents there are in existence which affect the title to the land. Now Lord Hardwick decided [1] that a purchaser of land in Middlesex, having notice of a document affecting the land, was bound by it, although the document had not been registered according to the Middlesex Register Act; and a purchaser was thus rendered liable to be deprived of his purchase, through forgetfulness or some slight inadvertence on the part of himself or his agent. Lord Hardwick has been blamed for this decision, which went far to destroy the utility of the registers of Middlesex and Yorkshire.[2] The censure was, however, undeserved, as the decision was in accordance with the intention of the Act, as disclosed by the preamble.

As these Acts are acknowledged to be defective in allowing a purchaser to be affected by an unregistered document, I suggest that the defect should be removed, and an efficient system of registration made general throughout England.

I venture to propose that any one in possession of land, for a freehold estate, or leasehold estate of twenty-one years or upwards, should be entitled to have the land entered on the Register, upon paying the expense of surveying the boundaries, by an official surveyor; that the boundaries should be

[1] In Le Neve v. Le Neve, Amb. 436.
[2] The Yorkshire Acts have been amended by 47 & 48 Vict. c. 54.

marked on a copy of the ordnance map, so that by inspection, it might at once be ascertained whether a property had been registered or not.

When land had thus been registered, no purchaser or mortgagee should be affected by any dealing with the land, subsequent to the registration, which did not appear on the register; and further, every one dealing with the land should be considered as having notice of all that appeared on the register, whether he took the trouble of inspecting it or not.

For the purpose of registration a book might be appropriated to each registered property, so that by turning to that book, it might at once be known, with certainty, who had obtained any right in the property since the registration took place.

A claim as heir should be entered on the register, and after a certain period from the death of the owner, a *bonâ fide* purchaser, from one whose claim as heir has been so entered on the register, should not be affected by the claim of any person as heir or as devisee not registered previously to the purchase.

A will affecting the land should be entered on the register, and after a certain period from the decease of the testator, a *bonâ fide* purchaser from a devisee under such will, should not be affected by any will or claim as heir not previously registered.

The registration of any document or claim would not give to the document or claim itself any greater validity than it possessed before registration; the registration would simply prevent the validity of the document or claim (supposing a purchase or mortgage to have taken place on the faith of it) from being affected by documents or claims not previously registered, or by subsequent transactions.

If a registered property were divided, a new book referring to the old one should be appropriated to each portion. If several registered properties were consolidated, only one new book would be required for the whole, the new one referring to the books relating to the separate properties.

The map on which the registered properties were delineated would form the key and index to the volumes of registration; each property would receive a number, and this number would constitute a sufficient description of the property in conveyances, mortgages, &c.

It seems to me clear, that after the lapse of a few years, through the operation of the Statute of Limitations, an indefeasible title would be obtained under such a system of registration, without the expense and danger of an official investigation of titles, and that equitable rights would, as well as legal rights, be perfectly protected.

In order to preserve the facilities which landowners now enjoy, of creating a security by the deposit of title-deeds, I would propose that any one, who appears by the register to be entitled to an interest in the land, should, on application, be furnished with a certificate that he appears by the register to be entitled to such interest, and the fact of the certificate being granted should be entered on the register. After this, any one dealing with the same interest should be held bound by any right secured by the deposit of the certificate. It would, therefore, in order to deal safely with the interest, be necessary that the certificate should be produced and handed over to a purchaser or mortgagee, or entered on the register as surrendered.

In the subsequent chapters will be found a short examination of the two modern Registration Acts.

III.

MODERN REGISTRATION ACTS.

25 & 26 Vict. c. 53.

As REGARDS the two modern attempts to establish a system of registration, it appears to have been the principal object of the first, the 25 & 26 Vict. c. 53 (1862), that the owner of land should be enabled to obtain an absolutely indefeasible title to his property. Now, desirable as is this object, it is one which cannot be attained without a minute investigation into the actual title. In order not to commit injustice by destroying the right of an absent and, it may be, an unknown person, it is absolutely necessary to ascertain that the applicant, who requires the grant of an indefeasible title, is the true and sole owner; and this cannot be effected without a rigid examination of documents, and public advertisements limiting a time for adverse claimants to come in—precautions which necessarily occasion considerable delay and expense. Owners, therefore, who feel satisfied with their titles, as practically, if not theoretically, sufficient, have been unwilling to apply, at this cost, for an indefeasible title; while in cases where some doubts existed respecting the perfection of the title, the owner has been fearful of submitting it to the strict preliminary scrutiny. Hence the Act had little practical value, except in cases where a considerable property was to be disposed of by dividing it into numerous lots. In such a case registration under this Act might effect a saving of expense, besides giving an indefeasible title to the purchasers.

Criticism would, however, be wasted on the provisions of this Statute, since the registration under it was closed (after a trial of thirteen years) by the 38 & 39 Vict. c. 87, the Registration Act at present in force.

IV.

THE PRESENT GENERAL REGISTRATION ACT.

THE objections which I pointed out, as having been fatal to the usefulness of the former Act, apply also to the present (the Land Transfer Act, 1875. 38 & 39 Vict. c. 87), viz., the expense and possible danger which must be incurred in order to obtain registration. An indisputable title, subject or not subject to specified qualifications, cannot be granted without the rigid investigation requisite to prove that there exist no valid latent claims.

Nor is it clear that the advantages to be derived from the possession of an indisputable title under the Act are such as to counterbalance these objections.

The object of the Act appears to be the assimilation, as far as practicable, of the method of conveying land to that which is in force for transferring Government stock.

If stock is entered in the books kept by the Bank of England in the name of one or more persons, the stock becomes, at law, the absolute property of those persons or person, so far as the books convey information. You are not allowed to enter in these books the name of a person as having merely a limited interest, for example an interest for life, in a sum of stock.

So under the present Land Act (putting leaseholds out of the question), a person can be registered as owner of an absolute estate or fee-simple only. If a life interest is to be conferred, it must be given by way of trust; the person registered as owner in fee must execute an instrument declaring that he holds the land in trust for the person designated, for his life—the Act not making any provision for the registration of trusts.

As the Bank of England will not take notice of any trust of stock, the new register, like the Bank books, is a register of absolute owners. The Act, however, permits the registration of money charges on registered land.

Hitherto a provision (say for infant children) out of land, has been considered more secure than a provision out of stock. The latter is at the mercy of a trustee. The purchaser of stock from a trustee, in whose name the stock stands, is safe, in the absence of notice of the trust, and the person beneficially entitled has no remedy except against the trustee personally. A trust estate in land could not without difficulty be defeated by a sale, because a purchaser of the land would, almost necessarily, have notice of the trust—the trustee in establishing his own title would disclose the trust also. Even if the land were vested in trustees for sale, the almost necessary notoriety of the sale of unregistered land affords practical protection to the beneficial owner.

As regards land registered under this Act the case will be different. The person who is registered owner can convey the land discharged of all trusts, except registered money charges, by a transaction no more notorious than a transfer of Government stock.

It is true that the Act provides for the entry of "cautions" on the register, and when a caution has been entered, the land is not to be dealt with, until notice of the intended transfer has been given personally, or by post, to the cautioners—a proceeding analogous to placing a distringas on stock at the Bank of England. But, although the notice is not duly given, the sale is still absolute—and in many instances beneficial owners, especially if they are infants, will omit to enter a caution.

It is, perhaps, unnecessary to remark, that the security at present enjoyed by partial owners of land as, for example, tenants for life, entitled at law will be much diminished if the land is registered under this Act, because the interest of such an owner will be necessarily converted into an equitable interest.

Nor is this all; by the 41st Section if a person registered as sole owner of freehold land (or the survivor of several registered owners) dies, the land which he held will not pass to his heir, or to his personal representatives, but to a person nominated by the Registrar, at his discretion, regard being had to the rights of persons interested in the land. So that if the deceased was the beneficial owner, his heir, widow, or the devisees under his will, may find their interests in the land at the mercy of a person, whom neither they nor the deceased had any potential voice in selecting, and who may defeat their rights by a sale and transfer on the register to a purchaser, whether that person had or had not notice of the trusts. (See Section 30.)

It may well be asked with what view are these provisions with regard to Registration introduced? They will clearly have the effect of rendering less secure the interests of many persons in landed property, supposing the land to be registered under the Act. What then are the countervailing advantages which the authors of the Act expect that it will confer?

I have heard it stated by a high authority that the late Mr. Cobden declared, after having attained free trade in corn, that the next most important object was, in his opinion, to establish free trade in land. I do not feel sure as to the meaning which he attached to this expression; but I presume that "establishing free trade in land" means providing for its purchase and sale in the same manner as Government and other stocks and securities are purchased and sold in the market.

The authors of the Act under consideration appear to have had this object in view. The persons in whose names land is registered are to be the absolute owners (not owners for life or in remainder), in the same sense that proprietors of Government stock are absolute owners. The directors of the Bank of England, who have charge of the national stocks, as well as of their own, refuse to take notice of trusts— the Registrar of land is to do the same. The cautions which may be entered on the register are apparently devised in imitation of the distringas which may be placed upon Government stocks.

To a landowner engaged in commercial speculations, it may be advantageous to register his land under the Act. The registration might render it more easy for him to raise money on the security of his estate, or to sell it with despatch, on an emergency. He might, perhaps, have his land quoted like so much stock, and make it a subject of speculation in the market. If many estates were thus offered for public sale, there might be called into existence a body of land-brokers and land-jobbers, who would benefit by land speculations; but I see no reason to suppose that, by such transactions, the cultivation of the soil would be improved. How could free trade in land produce effects at all analogous to the results of free trade in corn? Suppose that Bowood or Belvoir was registered by their proprietor, and thereby rendered more marketable, would a purchaser for a rise of one-eighth per cent. be likely to lay out capital in improving land which he intended to retain as his property only, it may be, till next settling day, or until he closed his speculation? Would he make a drain, or plant a tree—

"Seris
Umbram factura nepotibus?"

If it was not the object of the Act to encourage speculation in land, by assimilating land to Government stock, it is difficult to understand why the assimilation was attempted at all. Merely to facilitate *bonâ fide* investments in land, desirable as such an object is in itself, would not justify the introduction of a system of registration which diminishes the security of equitable interests, and prevents the creation of many legal estates which can be created in non-registered lands.

I will conclude this chapter by quoting an instance of the mode in which the antiquated system of land tenure, favouring the continuance of land in the same family for several generations, not unfrequently worked. The following statement is extracted from the *Times* of the 6th March, 1882, and relates to the Swinton estate in the North Riding of Yorkshire:—

"The rental is very considerable, amounting to

over 12,000*l.*, exclusive of the mansion, the park, and the grouse-shooting; yet relatively the superficial area is much in excess of the rent-roll.

. . . . .

"The bounds of Swinton are almost identical with those of the famous old manor of Mashamshire. Besides the thriving little market town of Masham, they include, either entirely or in part, several parishes, with sundry villages. And Mashamshire recalls a long train of historical associations, going back to Saxon times. It was owned at the Conquest by Earl Edwin, twin brother of Morcar, grandson of the great Leofric of Mercia and the Lady Godiva, and brother-in-law of the unfortunate Harold. The Conqueror confiscated it for the benefit of his nephew, the Earl of Bretagne and Richmond. In the reign of the first Edward it had passed to the Scropes, who were ennobled as Lords Scrope of Masham; and from the Scropes it came by marriage to the old Yorkshire family of the Danbys, whose descendants held it down to the present day.

. . . .

"Swinton is emphatically an 'old' property, as one of the people with whom I conversed on the estate remarked very suggestively. He meant that for generations it had been the pride of its owners; that they had lavished their money freely on it; and, indeed, everywhere you see signs that nothing has been stinted either in ornamental outlay or for remunerative improvements. The Danbys seem always to have resided at home, spending a large and unencumbered income in their parishes; they have been liberal landlords to an industrious tenantry, and I believe that in the last fifty years the rents have hardly been altered. Considering the rugged character of the country, there was ample scope for extending cultivation.

"Swinton may be supposed to have taken its name from the wild swine that, in the olden time, found inaccessible retreats in its woods and swampy wastes, and in the recesses of the precipitous ravines that everywhere intersect them.

"The father of the late Mr. Danby was a famous improver; so much so, that Arthur Young was induced to pay Swinton a visit on his 'Northern Tour.' Young, who was much gratified by what he saw, remarks that 'Mr. Danby possessed several thousands of contiguous acres, which did not yield him a tenth part as many farthings a year.' Those barren acres, where they have not been reclaimed, are now let to the sheep farmers; while as well-stocked grouse shootings, they, of course, have a value which was not dreamed of in 1768. That Mr. Danby's son, during his long occupation, seems to have improved almost as indefatigably as his father: he made many excellent roads, and built sundry substantial bridges, while he showed his admirable taste by judiciously beautifying the home domains."

The Danbys were clearly not traders in land. Is there any reason to believe that, had they been such, the lands of Masham would have been better cultivated, the plantations more extensive, or the inhabitants more prosperous and contented than they have become under the old system of land tenure?

THE END.

LONDON: RICHARD CLAY AND SONS, PRINTERS.

Now publishing, in Crown 8vo., price 3s. 6d. each volume.

The English Citizen:
A SERIES OF SHORT BOOKS ON
HIS RIGHTS AND RESPONSIBILITIES.
Edited by HENRY CRAIK, M.A., LL.D.

This series is intended to meet the demand for accessible information on the ordinary conditions and the current terms of our political life.

The volumes deal with the details of the machinery whereby our Constitution works and the broad lines upon which it has been constructed. The books are intended to select and sum up the salient features of any branch of legislation, so as to place the ordinary citizen in possession of the main points of the law.

The following are the titles of the Volumes:—

1. **Central Government.** H. D. Traill, D.C.L., late Fellow of St. John's College, Oxford.

   "A clear, straightforward style enables him to put his knowledge in a way at once concise and lucid."—*Saturday Review.*

2. **The Electorate and the Legislature.** Spencer Walpole, Author of "The History of England from 1815."

   "Mr. Walpole traces the growth of the power of Parliament through all those stages with which we are now familiar, and he does so very clearly and succinctly."—*St. James's Gazette.*

3. **Local Government.** M. D. Chalmers, M.A., Barrister-at-Law.

   "It is packed full of facts about our local government all worthy to be known."—*Saturday Review.*

4. **The National Budget: The National Debt,** TAXES, AND RATES. A. J. Wilson.

   "It is calculated to do much in the way of enlightenment."—*The Citizen.*

5. **The State in its Relation to Education.** Henry Craik, M.A. Oxon., LL.D. Glasgow.

   "An excellent digest of the progress of our national education during the present century."—*The Academy.*

6. **The Poor Law.** Rev. T. W. Fowle, M.A.

   "Mr. Fowle's treatise is a valuable little summary. . . . It is worthy of a wide circulation."—*The Academy.*

7. **The State in its Relation to Trade.** Sir T. H. Farrer, Bart.

   "The subject is one of which Sir T. H. Farrer, from his official position, speaks with a fulness of knowledge such as few possess, and this knowledge he has the faculty of conveying to others in a vigorous and attractive way."—*The Economist.*

8. **The State in Relation to Labour.** W. Stanley Jevons, LL.D., M.A., F.R.S.

   "This little book is full of useful information, well and thoughtfully digested."—*Law Times.*

9. **The Land Laws.** F. Pollock, Barrister-at-law, M.A., Hon. LL.D. Edin.; Corpus Christi Professor of Jurisprudence in the University of Oxford; late Fellow of Trinity College, Cambridge.

   "The excellence of the book as a survey of its subject can hardly be too well spoken of."—*Saturday Review.*

THE ENGLISH CITIZEN (*continued*).

10. The State and the Church. Hon. ARTHUR ELLIOT, M.P.
"This is an excellent work—judicious, candid, and impartial."—*North British Daily Mail.*

11. Foreign Relations. SPENCER WALPOLE, Author of "The History of England from 1815."
"A work which every student of public affairs should almost know by heart."—*Glasgow News.*

12. Colonies and Dependencies:
(1) INDIA. J. S. COTTON, late Fellow of Queen's College, Oxford.
(2) THE COLONIES. E. J. PAYNE, Fellow of University College, Oxford.
"One of the most interesting of this most valuable series."—*The Statist.*

13. Justice and Police. By F. W. MAITLAND.
"Is a very clear and concise exposition of a vast subject."—*Athenæum.*

14. The Punishment and Prevention of Crime. By Colonel Sir EDMUND DU CANE, K.C.B., R.E.
"Sir Edmund Du Cane's little volume, just published, on 'Punishment and Prevention of Crime,' gives an interesting account of the state of the criminal law as it has been and as it now is: of the objects which it has been framed to secure; of the methods resorted to, and of the degree of success by which they have been severally attended."—*Times.*

IN PREPARATION.

The National Defences. By Lieutenant-Colonel MAURICE, R.A.

Now Publishing, in Crown 8vo, price 2s. 6d. each. Also in stiff boards, uncut edges, price 2s. 6d. each.

ENGLISH MEN OF LETTERS.
EDITED BY JOHN MORLEY.

"These excellent biographies should be made class-books for schools."
—*Westminster Review.*
"This admirable series."—*British Quarterly Review.*
"Enjoyable and excellent little books."—*Academy.*

JOHNSON. By LESLIE STEPHEN.
SCOTT. By R. H. HUTTON.
GIBBON. By J. C. MORISON.
SHELLEY. By J. A. SYMONDS.
HUME. By T. H. HUXLEY, P.R.S.
GOLDSMITH. By WILLIAM BLACK.
DEFOE. By W. MINTO.
BURNS. By Principal SHAIRP.
SPENSER. By R. W. CHURCH, Dean of St. Paul's.
THACKERAY. By ANTH. TROLLOPE.
BURKE. By JOHN MORLEY.
MILTON. By MARK PATTISON.
HAWTHORNE. By HENRY JAMES.
SOUTHEY. By EDWARD DOWDEN.
CHAUCER. By A. W. WARD.
COWPER. By GOLDWIN SMITH.
BUNYAN. By J. A. FROUDE.
BYRON. By JOHN NICHOL.
LOCKE. By THOMAS FOWLER.
POPE By LESLIE STEPHEN.

CHARLES LAMB. By Rev. ALFRED AINGER.
DE QUINCEY. By DAVID MASSON.
LANDOR. By SIDNEY COLVIN.
DRYDEN. By GEORGE SAINTSBURY.
WORDSWORTH By F. W. H. MYERS.
BENTLEY. By Prof. R. C. JEBB.
SWIFT. By LESLIE STEPHEN.
DICKENS. By A. W. WARD.
GRAY. By EDMUND GOSSE.
STERNE. By H. D. TRAILL.
MACAULAY. By J. C. MORISON.
SHERIDAN. By Mrs. OLIPHANT.
FIELDING. By AUSTIN DOBSON.
ADDISON. By W. J. COURTHOPE.
BACON. By R. W. CHURCH, Dean of St. Paul's.
COLERIDGE. By H. D. TRAILL.
KEATS. By SIDNEY COLVIN.
[*In the press.*]

*** *Other Volumes to follow.*

MACMILLAN AND CO., LONDON.

MESSRS. MACMILLAN & CO.'S PUBLICATIONS.

WORKS BY THE RT. HON. HENRY FAWCETT, F.R.S.,
Late Professor of Political Economy at Cambridge.

Manual of Political Economy. Sixth Edition, revised, with a chapter "On State Socialism and the Nationalisation of the Land," and an Index. Crown 8vo. 12s.

Speeches on some Current Political Questions. 8vo. 10s. 6d.

CONTENTS:—Indian Finance—The Birmingham League—Nine Hours Bill—Election Expenses—Women's Suffrage—Household Suffrage in Counties—Irish University Education, &c.

Free Trade and Protection. An Inquiry into the Causes which have retarded the general adoption of Free Trade since its Introduction into England. Sixth and Cheaper Edition. Crown 8vo. 3s. 6d.

Indian Finance. Three Essays. With Introduction and Appendix. 8vo. 7s. 6d.

WORKS BY MILLICENT GARRETT FAWCETT.

Political Economy for Beginners, with Questions. Sixth Edition. 18mo. 2s. 6d.

Tales in Political Economy. Crown 8vo. 3s.

Essays and Lectures on Political and Social Subjects. By Right Hon. HENRY FAWCETT, and MILLICENT GARRETT FAWCETT. 8vo. 10s. 6d.

WORKS BY HENRY SIDGWICK, M.A., LL.D.,
Knightbridge Professor of Moral Philosophy in the University of Cambridge.

The Methods of Ethics. Third Edition, revised throughout, with Important Additions. 8vo. 14s.

A SUPPLEMENT to the Second Edition, containing all the important Additions and Alterations in the Third Edition. Demy 8vo. 6s.

The Principles of Political Economy. 8vo. 16s.

The Law of the Constitution, Lectures Introductory to the Study of. By A. V. DICEY, B.C.L., of the Inner Temple, Barrister-at-law. Vinerian Professor of English Law in the University of Oxford, Fellow of All Souls' College, Hon. LL.D., Glasgow. Demy 8vo, 12s. 6d.

MACMILLAN AND CO., LONDON.

MESSRS. MACMILLAN & CO.'S PUBLICATIONS.

WORKS BY FRANCIS A. WALKER, M.A., Ph.D.,
Professor of Political Economy and History, Sheffield Scientific School of Yale College; late Chief of the U.S. Bureau of Statistics, &c., &c.

The Wages Question. A Treatise on Wages and the Wages Class. 8vo. 14s.

Money. 8vo. 16s.

Money in its Relation to Trade and Industry. Crown 8vo. 7s. 6d.

Political Economy. 8vo. 10s. 6d.

Land and its Rent. Fcap. 8vo. 3s. 6d.

The Present Position of Economics. An Inaugural Lecture given in the Senate House at Cambridge on February 24, 1885. By ALFRED MARSHALL, M.A., Professor of Political Economy in the University of Cambridge; late Fellow of Balliol College, Oxford, &c. Crown 8vo. 2s.

The Economics of Industry. By ALFRED MARSHALL, M.A., Professor of Political Economy in the University of Cambridge, &c., and MARY PALEY MARSHALL, late Lecturer at Newnham Hall, Cambridge. Extra fcap. 8vo. 2s. 6d.

Annals of Our Time. A Diurnal of Events, Social and Political, Home and Foreign, from the Accession of Queen Victoria to the Peace of Versailles, 28th February, 1871. By JOSEPH IRVING. New Edition, revised. 8vo, half-bound. 18s.

Annals of Our Time. Supplement. From February 1871 to March 1874. Second Edition. 8vo. 4s. 6d.

Annals of Our Time. Supplement. From March 1874 to July 1878. 8vo. 4s. 6d.

Statesman's Year Book, The. A Statistical and Historical Annual of the States of the Civilised World for the year 1885. Twenty-second Annual Publication. Revised after Official Returns. Edited by J. SCOTT KELTIE. Crown 8vo. 10s. 6d.

Pleas of the Crown for the County of Gloucester BEFORE THE ABBOT OF READING AND HIS FELLOW JUSTICES ITINERANT, IN THE FIFTH YEAR OF THE REIGN OF KING HENRY THE THIRD, AND THE YEAR OF GRACE 1221. Edited by F. W. MAITLAND. 8vo. 7s. 6d.

MACMILLAN AND CO., LONDON.

www.ingramcontent.com/pod-product-compliance
Lightning Source LLC
Chambersburg PA
CBHW022147160426
43197CB00009B/1456